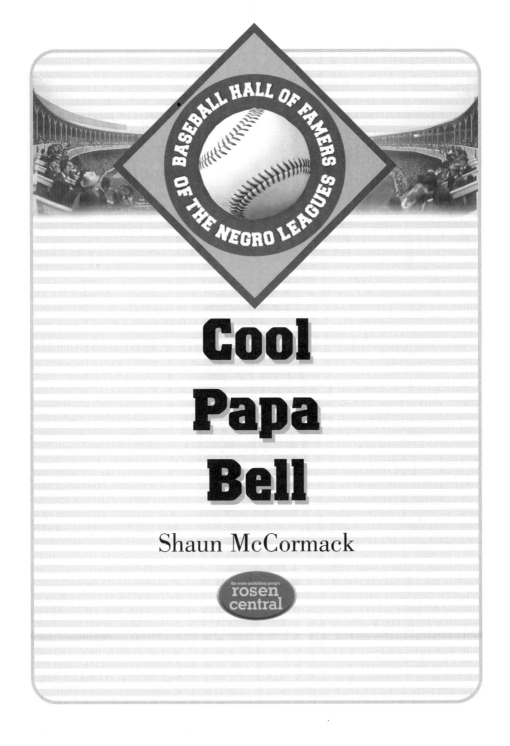

BASEBALL HALL OF FAMERS OF THE NEGRO LEAGUES

Cool Papa Bell

Shaun McCormack

the rosen publishing group's
rosen central

I would like to dedicate this book to my grandfather, Peter Roccagli. Without him, I would never have fully appreciated the game of baseball.

Published in 2002 by The Rosen Publishing Group, Inc.
29 East 21st Street, New York, NY 10010

First Edition

Library of Congress Cataloging-in-Publication Data

McCormack, Shaun.
Cool Papa Bell / Shaun McCormack.— 1st ed.
p. cm. — (Baseball Hall of Famers of the Negro Leagues)
Includes bibliographical references and index.
ISBN 0-8239-3474-8 (lib. bdg.)
1. Bell, Cool Papa, 1903–1991. 2. Baseball players—United States—
Biography. 3. Afro-American baseball players—Biography.
4. Negro leagues—History.
I. Title. II. Series.
GV865.B343 M33 2001
796.357'092—dc21

2001003121

Manufactured in the United States of America

Contents

Although the integration of major league baseball came too late for James "Cool Papa" Bell, his achievements as both a player and coach in the Negro leagues secured his induction into the Baseball Hall of Fame.

Introduction

Back in the 1950s and 1960s, a struggling Negro league baseball team, the Indianapolis Clowns, used to warm up in pantomime. They hurled a make-believe ball from the pitcher's mound toward home plate. Batters would hit ground balls with make-believe baseball bats and sprint down the baseline. Infielders would dash toward the imaginary ball, scoop it up bare-handed, and fire to first, narrowly beating runners at the first-base bag.

Sometimes the silent crack of the bat launched balls into the sky. Outfielders blocked the sun from their eyes, sprinted after invisible fly balls, and made dramatic diving catches on the outfield grass. All of this was done so convincingly that fans had a hard time believing that what they were seeing wasn't real.

The game was called shadowball.

Some sports historians have used the game shadowball as a metaphor for the kind of game played by Negro league baseball players from the late 1800s until the first African American man broke baseball's color barrier in 1946. Writers have used it as the title for books about baseball's Negro leagues. For nearly fifty years, black men played in the shadows of their white contemporaries. To this day, several black men who equaled and outdid the efforts of major league Hall of Fame legends are unknown and underappreciated.

Despite the fact that these players were unjustly barred from the big leagues, they played ball. They formed all-black baseball teams. They worked together with businessmen and the black community and organized the Negro leagues. This gave black ballplayers an opportunity to play organized baseball. Talented players surfaced in the leagues, and fans came to watch them showcase their talent.

The Negro leagues grew, strengthened, and emerged from the shadows during the 1930s and 1940s. The Negro leagues are an important part of American history. The best African American ball clubs, like the Pittsburgh Crawfords and Homestead Grays, were led by legends like James "Cool Papa" Bell, Satchel Paige, Josh Gibson, and others. These clubs were able to rise above the major league teams they were barred from playing against in end-of-the-year, barnstorming rivalries. Time after time, in thousands of hard-fought games, the players of the Negro leagues proved themselves the equal of or better than the big league players, and revealed what American baseball fans were losing as a result of segregated teams.

President Abraham Lincoln, who signed the Emancipation Proclamation in 1863, reads a Bible that was presented to him by Baltimore's black community. Former slave and abolitionist Sojourner Truth sits by his side.

Jim Crow Baseball

James Thomas Bell, who many have said was the fastest man ever to play the game of baseball, played at a time when African American ballplayers and teams were barred from participating in what were then the all-white professional baseball leagues.

Bell was born on May 17, 1901, near Starkville, Mississippi, into a farming community of about 2,700 people. It was less than fifty years since the Civil War had ended. African American slaves had been freed by the Emancipation Proclamation and the Thirteenth Amendment, but their lives were still lived under the shadows of poverty, discrimination, segregation, and racism.

Bell's father, Jonas Bell, sharecropped cotton and corn. Mary Nichols, his Native American mother, performed odd jobs in and around their farming community. James lived with his mother and father, two sisters, and five brothers on a farm a few miles from Starkville. He attended Starkville's segregated, one-room elementary school through the seventh grade.

James's elementary school, along with almost all facilities provided to African Americans in the post–Civil War South, was segregated from the schools attended by white boys and girls. "Separate but equal" was the term used to justify Jim Crow laws. These laws called for segregated schools, bathrooms, libraries, and other public facilities. Although slavery was now illegal, white America's acceptance of blacks as equals was slow in coming. The segregated public facilities provided for African Americans were usually inferior in quality to the white facilities. In reality, the term "separate and unequal" would have been more appropriate.

Jim Crow laws restored the inferior status of African Americans after the Civil War ended in 1865. Jim Crow laws were the written code that blocked emancipated slaves from the rights and privileges given to whites. Blacks and whites could not sit together on buses, on trains, or in restaurants. They were forbidden from drinking from the same water fountains. By 1900, Jim Crow laws had cast a shadow over the game of baseball.

In the late 1800s and early 1900s, Georgia passed legislation that read, "It shall be unlawful for any amateur white baseball team to play baseball on any vacant lot or baseball diamond within two blocks of a playground devoted to the Negro race, and it shall be unlawful for any amateur colored baseball team to play baseball in any vacant lot or baseball diamond within two blocks of any playground devoted to the white race." This meant not only that blacks and whites couldn't play together but also that they couldn't even play anywhere near each other.

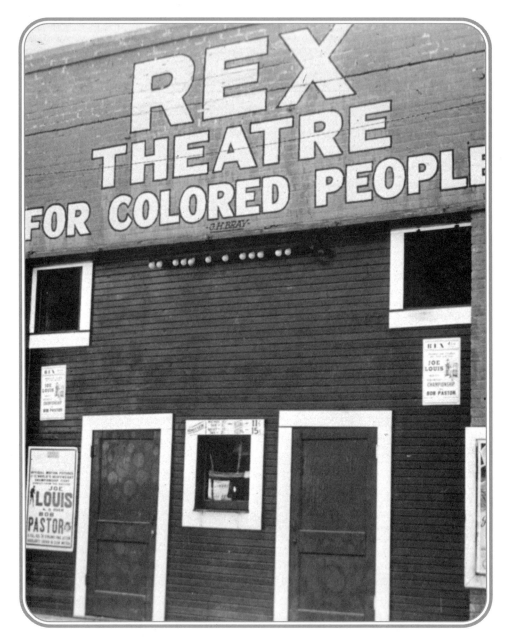

Jim Crow laws ensured the separation of the races in almost all aspects of life, including entertainment. The marquee of this segregated theater in Leland, Mississippi, is marked "For Colored People."

As early as 1867, the nominating committee of the National Association of Baseball Players drew baseball's color line. The committee unanimously came out against "the admission of any club which may be composed of one or more colored persons." The NABBP eventually disbanded, but its successor, the National Association of Professional Base Ball Players, upheld baseball's racist philosophy with an unwritten rule that barred African Americans from its teams and leagues. This racist exclusion is what brought the Negro leagues into existence.

By the year 1900, there were five all-black professional teams: the Cuban Giants, whose home city varied from year to year; the New York Cuban X Giants; the Norfolk, Virginia, Red Stockings; the Chicago Unions; and the Chicago Colombian Giants. African American teams flourished in the North and Midwest. By 1906, nine African American teams had surfaced within 100 miles of Philadelphia.

In 1910, the first effort was made to establish a Negro league that included teams from all over the country—from Chicago, Louisville, New Orleans, St. Louis, Kansas City, and Columbus. African American baseball leaders said they would pay up to $300 each for a franchise in the league. Unfortunately, the attempt dwindled before the league played its first game, and it would take another ten years before the first strong Negro league was established.

Tens of thousands of former slaves picked up their belongings and headed north every year in the early 1900s. By 1916, there were professional African American teams in almost every large city in the North and West. The Duval Giants of Jacksonville, Florida, also made the trip in 1916. Because there was little opportunity for an all-black ball club in the South at that time, the entire team picked up and headed north. They changed their name to the Bacharach Giants and settled in Atlantic City, New Jersey.

During this time, semipro and indep Negro leagues were born and died each y James Bell headed north in 1920. He settled in St. Louis, where some of his brothers were living and playing baseball.

That was the same year that the first viable Negro league—the Negro National League—was born. It began with eight teams: the Chicago American Giants, the Indianapolis ABCs, the Chicago Giants, the Kansas City Monarchs, the St. Louis Giants, the Detroit Stars, the Dayton Marcos, and the Cuban Stars. Owners of each team paid $500 to join the league. Many teams took the name of the Giants because it was at this time that major league baseball's New York Giants had become very successful. Many African American teams used "Cuban" or "Colombian" in their names to avoid discrimination. They believed Americans would be more tolerant of Central American players than African American players.

Andrew "Rube" Foster, the manager of the Chicago American Giants, is given credit for

Some Negro league teams, such as the Cuban Stars, were named after Caribbean and Central American countries in an effort by their owners to avoid discrimination against their black members.

Playing Against the Majors

Cool Papa Bell has often been called "the Black Ty Cobb." In 1910, Hall of Fame speedster Ty Cobb and his Detroit Tigers played twelve games against a Negro all-star team. The Tigers went 7–4 and tied one of the exhibition games. In 1915, major league teams played a series of eight exhibition games against African American teams. Many end-of-the-season "barnstorming" exhibition games made it plain to see that there were many African Americans gifted with the abilities to compete in the major leagues, but the color line was not broken until half a century later.

starting the Negro National League. His efforts earned him a spot in the National Baseball Hall of Fame. Foster suggested that the Negro National League fashion itself after the major leagues. Part of his effort was dedicated to ensuring that players didn't betray their teams in the middle of a season. Many teams were damaged when their players quit. Foster sought to establish a more civilized game. This idea didn't always play out the way Foster wanted. Many players—especially Bell's teammate Satchel Paige—did skip games, break contracts, and ditch their teams when the owners of other teams offered them more money.

In 1920, when Bell set out for St. Louis, he followed many African Americans who already had left the South's rural Mississippi River Valley communities for urban hubs in the Midwest. The men who had gone before him brought their music—the Delta blues—and their baseball with them. All-black semipro and professional teams were beginning to flourish. They were beginning to compete against all-white semipro and major league teams. Bell went to St. Louis with the hope of making a better life for himself.

Bell eventually found himself settling in St. Louis for about ten years. He said of the city: "You could just live better and make more money" there. This is where Bell made his entrance into baseball's Negro leagues. He

Three members of the Delta Rhythm Boys, a quintet of Delta blues singers, harmonize during a live radio performance in the 1940s. Musicians and ballplayers, as well as thousands of other African Americans, went north to make better lives for themselves.

joined an all-black semipro team, the
Compton Hill Cubs. Bell played for the team
on Sundays and holidays.

Bell earned a name for himself with his
keen hitting skills, blazing speed, and
dazzling center field performance, but with
the Compton Hill Cubs the five-foot-eleven,
145-pound Bell signed on as a knuckleball
pitcher. With his knuckleball, Bell had a
pitch to baffle batters. When throwing the
pitch, he would wind up and release the
baseball so that it left his hand without any
rotation on it. Knuckleballs are thrown softly.
Good ones dance around chaotically before
reaching the batter. Bad ones have very little
movement. Without movement, they are very
easy to hit.

While hurling knuckleballs for the Compton
Hill Cubs, Bell was earning a modest $21.20
per week laboring at the Independent Packing
Company. He attended high school at night. In
August of 1921, the Compton Hill Cubs
disbanded. Bell then joined another semipro

team, the East St. Louis Cubs, in 1922. With his new team, Bell earned $20 per week for his pitching performances on Sundays.

That spring, Bell got his first big break. He tried out and made the cut for the St. Louis Stars, a powerhouse in the Negro National League. With the Stars, Bell was able to earn $90 per month. In 1922, his first full season with the Stars, Bell batted over .400 in about 60 at-bats. He slugged three doubles, a triple, and three home runs. While playing for the Stars, Bell hit well over .300 seven times. Records show he hit 15 home runs in 1926 and 11 of them in 1925.

Over the first twelve years of the Negro National League's existence, the Chicago American Giants were the strongest team. They were the only team that remained in the league for each of those years. The city of St. Louis was always represented in the league, but its club ownership changed hands. The St. Louis Giants franchise became the St. Louis Stars in 1921.

Scheduling games was always a problem because none of the teams could afford a home stadium. Many clubs signed deals to lease ballparks from white teams. Negro teams would play their home games when the white teams were on the road.

With these arrangements, it was almost impossible to create a schedule of games that would be fair to all clubs. Records show that it was rare for all teams to play the same number of games. In 1921, the Chicago American Giants won the championship for the second time. The Kansas City Monarchs, who came in second place that year, played 62 games. The last-place Chicago Giants were able to play only 42 games.

The St. Louis Stars improved almost immediately after Bell joined the team. In his first year, they won 23 and lost 23. By 1924, the team was much more competitive, winning 40 and losing 36. The Stars finished in second place in the first half of 1925 with a record of 31 and 14, trailing the mighty Kansas City

Monarchs, who finished at 31 and 9. But in the second half of that season, the Stars played better than the Monarchs. They won 38 games and lost 12. Finally, in a playoff for the Negro National League pennant, the Monarchs edged Bell's Stars 4 games to 3.

Oscar Charleston. Bell earned his nickname "Cool" after striking out this powerful and intimidating hitter.

The Fastest Player Ever?

Bell earned his famous nickname not for his speed around the bases and in center field, but for his calm approach to stressful situations. While playing with the Stars, it is said that he earned the nickname "Cool" after striking out feared Negro National League slugger Oscar Charleston in a crucial game situation.

There were plenty of reasons why Bell should have feared Charleston. First of all, the man was huge—six feet tall and nearly 200 pounds. Charleston was built like Babe Ruth and ran like Ty Cobb. Second, he was mean and loved to fight. There were five seasons in which Charleston was said to have hit over .400. His lifetime average was .357. One story says that Charleston once hit a ball so hard and so far over the fence that it made a pitcher cry.

Knowing all of this, Bell was able to dominate Charleston—getting him to swing and miss at his tricky knuckleballs. After this, Bell's teammates and opponents began calling him Cool, but Stars manager Bill Gatewood felt the name was incomplete. He tagged Papa on to the end of it, and the name stuck. To this day, Bell is known to the baseball world as Cool Papa, not James Thomas.

In the early stages of his career, Bell was primarily a pitcher and made only sporadic appearances in the outfield. In 1924, at Gatewood's recommendation, Bell began working harder on his fielding skills. He began seeing more and more playing time in center field. Gatewood was responsible for two changes in Bell's play that would prove to be very important to his success.

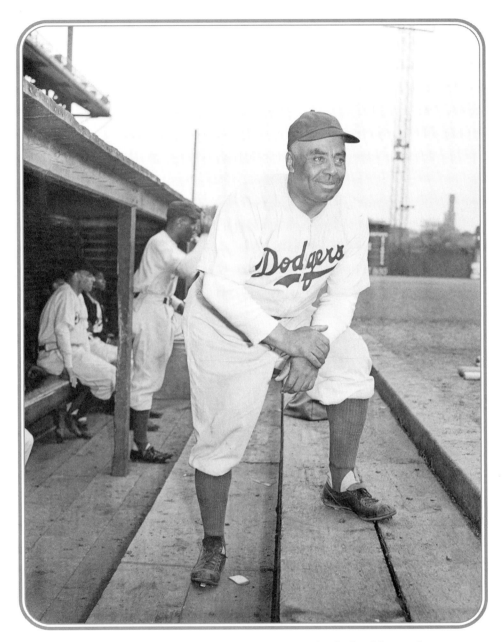

Negro league slugger Oscar Charleston, who had a lifetime batting average of .357, wound up playing for the Brooklyn Dodgers.

Bell scrapped his knuckleball and his pitching aspirations and began playing exclusively in center field. Next, he learned to bat from both sides of the plate. Bell had always been a right-handed batter and a southpaw, which means that he threw the baseball with his left hand. Because Bell was a southpaw, he was a valuable addition to any pitching rotation. Southpaws are rare. Two-thirds of major league pitchers are right-handed. Southpaws have proven year after year that they have a competitive edge against left-handed batters. To this day, left-handed hurlers are a hot commodity in the major leagues.

Gatewood pleaded with Bell and eventually convinced him to turn his talents to center field so that he could become an everyday player. Bell eventually became a defensive specialist— an all-star and eventual Hall of Famer—in center field. Learning to switch hit also helped to give Bell a few extra steps on infielders. When he batted from the left side, he started out a few feet closer to first base. It's impossible to tell just how much this helped him. It could have played a part in Bell legging out hundreds of his base hits.

Bell did not have the strongest arm in the league. This was evident from his pitching style. He had always relied on finesse and accuracy instead of a blazing fastball to get hitters out. What his arm lacked, however, his legs more than made up for. Bell's speed was unmatched. He was known for playing extremely shallow in center field. He was able to charge in to catch balls hit just over the heads of shortstops and second basemen in front of him. Even though he played shallow, baseballs rarely sailed past him. Cool Papa was able to sprint deep into the outfield from shallow center to make catches that would have sailed past many outfielders who played much deeper than he did.

Bell's fame began to grow shortly after he became a center fielder. He was playing every day now, so people were seeing a lot more of him. His base-running feats brought him the reputation of being the fastest player in baseball. Bell said himself that he stole 175 bases in 200 games during the 1933 season. He was able to taunt and distract pitchers once he reached base. This made it easier for the hitters that batted behind him in the lineup. The pitcher would be so worried about Bell stealing bases that his concentration would be lost. Bell was the prototypical lead-off hitter. To this day, major league baseball teams look for lead-off hitters that display the same types of skills that Bell had.

Owners and managers look for fast runners with a "good eye." Having a good eye means that the hitter is a good judge of balls and strikes. Good lead-off hitters usually have a high on-base percentage, which is the total number of walks and hits divided by the number of at-bats they have. They don't have to get base hits; they just have to get on base. A player with a high on-base percentage is valuable at the top of a lineup because he can get on base and set the stage for the sluggers in the middle of the lineup.

No one wanted to walk Bell because that would put him on first. He would usually be able to steal second and third base. If there was a base hit, Bell could usually score from first base. Allowing him to get on base was a tragedy for opposing pitchers. It usually meant that he would score.

It is said that Bell won the 1934 East-West Negro All-Star Game by drawing a walk and stealing second base in the eighth inning. Bell reportedly scored the game's only run on a soft hit by Jud Wilson of the Philadelphia Stars. Bell breezed around the bases, scoring easily from second base to secure a 1–0 victory for starting pitcher Satchel Paige and the East All-Stars. This happened again and again throughout his career. It is the main reason that he was such a dangerous player.

Several years later, in 1948, at the age of forty-five, Bell rounded the bases and scored from first on a sacrifice bunt in an exhibition barnstorming game against the American League's Cleveland Indians. Even in the twilight of his career, Bell could run with the best of them.

Bell ended up spending ten years with the St. Louis Stars. With Bell, shortstop Willie Wells—who was said to have been Bell's closest friend—and first baseman Mules Suttles, the Stars became a Negro National League powerhouse. The team contended for Negro National League championships in 1929 and 1930 against the mighty Kansas City Monarchs.

In the 1920s and 1930s, the art of "little ball," that is, advancing runners from base to base through base hits and bunting, rather than swinging for home runs, was losing importance in the major leagues. Babe Ruth had stormed onto the scene and gotten the league to focus on home runs. Why risk being gunned down trying for extra bases when the next batter might blast one over the fence? This was the all or nothing way of thinking that prevailed in the big leagues at the time.

Home runs were a big part of the Negro leagues as well, with sluggers like Josh Gibson

Willie Wells, shown here in a Memphis Red Sox uniform, was one of Cool Papa Bell's closest friends when the two played for the St. Louis Stars.

Josh Gibson of the Homestead Grays. Gibson was one of a number of powerful hitters who focused the game on home runs.

bashing baseballs over fences at will—if the field he played on even had a fence. But in the Negro leagues, little ball and baserunning still flourished. Drawing walks, stealing bases, bunting, sacrificing to move runners into scoring position, and hustling on every play still played big parts in Negro league baseball games. Speed was very important. And Cool Papa was the best at doing these things.

"We played a different kind of baseball than the white teams," Bell said. "We played tricky baseball. We did things they didn't expect. We'd bunt and run in the first inning. Then when they would come in for a bunt we'd hit away. We always crossed them up. We'd run the bases hard and make the fielders throw too quick and make wild throws. We'd fake a steal home and rattle the pitcher into a balk."

There were times when Bell would dash all the way in from center field to second base to catch a pick-off throw from the pitcher. According to Buck Leonard, a first baseman who batted behind Josh Gibson in the Homestead Grays' lineup, "Cool Papa Bell was about the best, and he was over the hill when I came up." Bill Yancey, a gifted shortstop who worked as a talent scout for the New York Yankees after playing for fourteen years in the Negro leagues, said:

I haven't seen anybody yet could run with Cool. When I was on the Lincoln Giants, we played in a little park in New York called the Catholic Protectory up in the Bronx. That was our regular home field. Judy Johnson had been telling me about this guy that came to Cuba every winter, and Judy told me, "if the guy hits the ball on two hops on the ground you won't be able to throw him out from shortstop."

Now I could throw, and I said nobody can outrun a baseball.

So the first time Cool Papa came to New York with the St. Louis Stars, he hit the ball into right field. Chino Smith was out there, and he could field a ball, and if you made a wide turn at first base he could throw you out trying to hustle back. I went out to get the throw, and when I looked up

Judy Johnson. Johnson, who often played with and against Cool
Papa Bell in winter ball matches in Cuba, admired Bell's speed
and base-running hustle.

Cool Papa was slowing up going into third. And I said to myself, "That sonofagun didn't touch second."

Some of Bell's contemporaries said that he was not only fast, but tricky, too. "You had to watch him on the bases," said Jack Marshall. "I saw him go from first to third and he never even touched second. He ran inside it by three feet when the umpire wasn't looking!"

But Yancey was still amazed by Bell's speed. "Next time up he hit another one about the same place. Now nobody got a three base hit in that little park, I don't care where they hit the ball. And I watched this guy run. Well, he came across second base and it looked like his feet weren't touching the ground! And he never argued, never said anything. That was why they called him Cool Papa; he was a real gentleman."

During Bell's prime, about a third of all major league players were from the South. They would not play with or against African Americans. African Americans could not travel with white major league clubs because many hotels would not accommodate them. Also, many baseball clubs held spring training in the South, where it was almost impossible for an African American to live peacefully. Organizations and hate groups like the Ku Klux Klan made life in the South miserable for African Americans.

Hate groups such as the Ku Klux Klan, seen here inducting a new member, continued to create problems for African Americans well into the 1960s.

The few African Americans who did play on white teams in white leagues before baseball's color line was officially drawn were often threatened. No matter how great their talent, owners and officials from Southern towns and cities would threaten teams that allowed African Americans to play with them. Racist Southerners, who refused to accept the fact that African Americans deserved the same rights that white men and women were given, feared losing to black teams.

3

Truth and Legend

Few Negro league baseball teams played traditional schedules or kept accurate statistics. For this reason, the achievements of Negro league players like Cool Papa Bell have survived mostly through storytelling and memories. The stories surrounding Cool Papa Bell's speed are some of the most unbelievable and interesting tales of all.

Bell himself said he once stole 175 bases in a 200-game season. There is some doubt he did this. The standard for excellence in today's game is 50 stolen bases in a season. Few players do it. Since baseball ended its last players strike in 1994, baseballs have been flying over the fence like crazy. Little ball and

Cool Papa Bell steals a base for the Homestead Grays. Opposing pitchers feared walking Bell because of his reputation as a quick and skilled base runner.

speed are again losing importance. Center fielder Ricky Henderson is the modern-day speed king. He has stolen 100 bases in a single 162-game season. To steal 175 bases in one year is an amazing feat.

Since Henderson accomplished this feat in the mid 1980s, few players have stolen even 50 bases. Since 1994, several players have hit more than 50 home runs in a single season. Mark McGwire in 1998 broke Roger Maris's thirty-eight-year single-season home run record by hitting 70 home runs. During that year, both he and Sammy Sosa had a season-long assault on Maris's record. Both of them surpassed this standard by the end of the season.

Baseball has again entered a home run era. Many baseball analysts say that the ball is "juiced," meaning that baseballs are manufactured differently so they can be hit farther. Others blame it on new baseball stadiums, which are much smaller than older ballparks. Because of expansion into new cities, the quality of pitching has declined.

Ricky Henderson is safe stealing second base for the New York Yankees—setting a Yankee record of 81 stolen bases—in a game against the Baltimore Orioles on September 15, 1986.

This has given sluggers the upper hand. They are able to prey on inexperienced or fading pitchers.

Fans love the drama associated with the home run, so it makes sense for owners to build their parks with shorter distances. The more home runs there are, the more fans there will be. More fans mean more ticket sales. This is the logic. If this trend continues, there may never again be another base stealer to come close to Bell's achievement of 175 stolen bases in a single season. Bell's accomplishment is hard to imagine, but some of the other tales associated with his game play stretch the imagination even further.

Legend has it that when Bell was in his prime, he was the fastest man alive. Bell's friend and teammate, Satchel Paige, said that Olympic running champion Jesse Owens refused to race Bell because he knew he would lose. Bell routinely scored from first base on base hits and once scored from first on a bunt when he was forty-five years old. He often made it from first to third on infield ground outs.

One story, which was told time and time again by Satchel Paige, was that Bell was so fast that he could flick the light switch off and be in bed before the room was dark. Bell actually once rigged the light switch in his hotel room while Paige was out. Bell rigged it so that the lights would remain on for two or three seconds after the switch was turned off. When Paige came back and got in his bed, Bell flicked the switch and jumped into his own bed—before the lights went out!

Infielders would yell frantically to each other and scramble in when Bell stepped to the plate. When he came up with two outs and no one on base, the infield would play extremely shallow, as if there was a runner at third with no outs. When there is a runner on third and less than two outs, coaches almost always bring the infield in so that the infielders have a chance to throw out the runner charging toward the plate. With the infield in, they are closer to home plate. The ball gets to them faster. But Bell forced managers to break convention. The infield would have to come in when he was up because they would not be able to throw him out at first if they played back. If Bell was on third with less than two outs, there was nothing that could stop him from scoring on a ground ball.

According to Jimmie Crutchfield, a teammate of Bell's on the Pittsburgh Crawfords, "[When] Bell hit one back to the pitcher, everybody would yell, 'Hurry!'" Teammate Judy Johnson said, "You couldn't play back in your regular position or you'd never throw him out." Before Jackie Robinson made it into the major leagues, Bell would often show him how it would be impossible for him to make it as a shortstop. Robinson had a weak throwing arm. He was not able to throw Bell out at first base if he had to range to his right to field a ground ball. Bell was just too fast for him.

Bell was supposed to have been able to circle the bases in twelve seconds flat. The official major league record is 13.3 seconds. It was set by Evar Swanswon of the National League's Cincinnati Reds in 1931. Bell is also credited with hitting .437 in 1940 for Torreon of the Mexican league. In 89 games that year, Bell led the league with 119 runs, 167 hits, 15 triples, 12 home runs, and 79 runs batted in. Some records show that he hit

Jimmie Crutchfield, Bell's teammate on the Pittsburgh Crawfords

.407 in 1944 and .402 in 1946. Other statistics show he hit as high as .490 in one year.

Many of Bell's achievements went unnoticed and unrecorded. "I remember one game I got five hits and stole five bases, but none of it was written down because they didn't bring the score book to the game that day," Bell said. It's impossible to tell how many bases he actually stole. One estimate says that he stole only 143

Bill Veeck of the Cleveland Indians was the first American League owner to sign an African American player.

bases throughout his professional career. Other accounts say that he had more than that in almost every season he played.

Bill Veeck of the Cleveland Indians said this about Bell: "Defensively, he was the equal of Tris Speaker, Joe DiMaggio, or Willie Mays." Speaker, DiMaggio, and Mays were some of the greatest men to ever play baseball. Baseball scout Eddie Gottlieb said, "If he had played in the major leagues, he would have reminded fans of Willie Keeler as a hitter and Ty Cobb as a base runner—and he might have exceeded both." Both Keeler and Cobb dominated baseball's early years.

Bell played on the Pittsburgh Crawfords for four years between 1933 and 1936 with legends Satchel Paige and Josh Gibson. With these superstars, the Crawfords won championships in 1933, 1935, and 1936.

Many say that Paige was the most talented pitcher to ever hurl a baseball. Bell certainly felt that he was one of the most dominating pitchers baseball has ever had. Paige was a showman as well, always wanting to entertain fans and make opponents look foolish. He had several names for his fastball, the "Bee Ball," the "Jump Ball," the "Trouble Ball," and the "Midnight Rider." Satchel was able to throw his fastball over ninety miles per hour. This is as fast as the fastballs pitched today by Randy Johnson and Pedro Martinez, two of baseball's most dominating pitchers. The thing that makes Satchel's fastball more impressive is that he threw it at a time when there was less science and physical training used in baseball.

It wasn't until late in his career, when Satchel was in his forties and fifties, that he developed a curveball. He had to because at that age his arm had lost some of its juice. Most power pitchers—the New York Yankees' Roger Clemens is a perfect example—lose something off their fastball late in their careers. The best pitchers are able to compensate for this by developing other pitches. Satchel was able to do this. By developing a number of off-speed pitches to keep hitters off balance, Satchel was

Satchel Paige of the Miami Marlins delivers a pitch during a game against the Montreal Royals on April 29, 1956.

able to finesse his way around batters and extend his incredibly long career.

Another pitch of Satchel's, the "Windmill," confused batters and was banned when he finally did make it into the major leagues. Satchel would wind his arm up several times, spinning it around behind him. Before hurling it toward the plate, he would lean back, and pause for a moment before unleashing it. When he did release the ball, it was supposed to travel so fast that batters could not see it.

One Negro leaguer, Biz Mackey, said that there were times when the ball Satchel threw simply vanished into thin air. "A lot of pitchers have a fastball, but a very, very few—Feller, Grove, Johnson, a couple of others besides Satchel—have had that little extra juice that makes the difference between the good and the great man. When it's that fast, it will hop a little at the end of the line," Mackey said.

Today, Boston's Pedro Martinez has a fastball that explodes before it reaches home plate. Martinez's fastball has been clocked at near 100 miles per hour. He has struck out as many as nineteen hitters in a single game—that's more than two strikeouts every inning. When Martinez throws his best fastball, it is almost impossible to hit. Batters need to swing before the ball is even released to catch up with a ball that fast. This is what Mackey meant when he described Paige's fastball.

Mackey said this about Satchel's best fastball as it approached the plate: "Beyond that, it tends to disappear. Yes, disappear. I've heard about Satchel throwing pitches that wasn't hit but that never showed up in the catcher's mitt nevertheless. They say the catcher, the umpire, and the bat boys looked all over for that ball, but it was gone. Now how do you account for that?"

On July 9, 1949, just after he turned forty-two years old, Satchel again became a rookie. Satchel became the first African American ever to pitch in the American League. He made a two-inning relief appearance for the Cleveland Indians in his major league debut.

That year, he pitched in twenty-one games as a reliever, winning six and losing one. Satchel is said to have pitched for African American barnstorming clubs through 1967, when he was sixty-one years old!

Records of his accomplishments after 1961 are very scarce. By 1961, when his book *Maybe I'll Pitch Forever* came out, Satchel estimated that he had pitched in more than 2,500 baseball games and won almost 2,000 of them. For three decades between 1929 and 1958, he pitched almost every day. He played during the summers in America and went down to the Dominican Republic, Cuba, or Mexico to spend his winters playing ball. Some days he played two or three games. Satchel claims he once pitched 153 games in a single year.

Throughout his career, Satchel pitched for about 250 teams. He barnstormed for many different teams one game at a time to earn extra money. Before getting his first shot in the majors, Satchel had pitched for the Pittsburgh Crawfords and Kansas City Monarchs, two of the Negro National League's most powerful ball clubs. Of all Negro league players, Satchel Paige was the best paid. It was probably a combination of his incredible talent and his willingness to entertain crowds.

Men who played with Satchel say he often told sportswriters that he was going to strike out the first six or nine men he faced in a game. Many times he kept his word. In other games, when his team was well ahead and had control of the game, he would call his outfield in, tell them to sit down, and then proceed to strike out the next batter. This flair for the dramatic is what helped Satchel earn up to $40,000 per year when he played with the Monarchs.

The accomplishments of Bell's Pittsburgh Crawfords teammate Josh Gibson also blurred the line between truth and legend. There is little doubt that Gibson was one of the mightiest sluggers ever to grace the baseball diamond. Many say he could hit more home runs—and longer ones—than legendary sluggers Babe Ruth, Hank Aaron, or Mark

Josh Gibson waits for his turn at bat during a Negro league game.

McGwire. Many record books show Gibson hit 962 home runs over his career. That is 200 more than Hank Aaron's official major league record.

It is also said that Gibson once hit 75 home runs in a single season, which is two more than the major league record, which Barry Bonds established in 2001. Gibson is supposed to have hit a ball completely out of Yankee Stadium. If this is true, it is the longest ball ever hit in the "House That Ruth Built," which is the stadium's nickname. Gibson's lifetime batting average was estimated to be .354.

Cool Papa Bell fields a ball for the Chicago American Giants during a Negro league game. The Giants were the last team he played for before retiring.

Glory and Peril

4

Throughout Bell's twenty-four-year career, his popularity was evident. Bell played for the Compton Hill Cubs, an amateur team, and the East St. Louis Cubs, a semipro team, before starting his professional career. Bell played for seven professional teams: the St. Louis Stars, the Homestead Grays, the Detroit Wolves, the Kansas City Monarchs, the Pittsburgh Crawfords, the Memphis Red Sox, and the Chicago American Giants. After retiring from professional ball he played for the Detroit Senators.

Bell was a participant in the East-West All-Star Game every year from its inception in 1933 through 1944, except for the years when he was playing in Latin America. His exceptional batting skills produced a .391 batting average in barnstorming exhibition games against major leaguers. The lowest estimate of his lifetime batting average is .341. In 1945, when he was past his prime and forty years old, Bell still ranked among the league leaders in stolen bases.

Other batting average estimates are higher. Some say his lifetime batting average was as high as .391 and that he batted over .400 several times in his career. He was not graced with the slugging power of contemporaries like Josh Gibson or Oscar Charleston, but what he lacked in power he made up for in speed. Bell was able to accumulate a high total of doubles and triples each year because of his quickness.

When compared to major leaguers, there is little doubt that he could have been one of the best at any level of competition. Hitting .400 is a phenomenal achievement. Ted Williams was the last player to hit over .400 in a season. He hit .406 in 1941. The Hall of Fame slugger

George Brett, who played for the American League's Kansas City Royals, hit .390 in 1980. Many people said that Tony Gwynn of the San Diego Padres, or Wade Boggs when he was in his prime playing for the Boston Red Sox, had the best chance of hitting .400, but neither of them ever did it. A few players, including the Colorado Rockies' Larry Walker, have flirted with .400 in the past five years, but many sports writers discount these achievements. It is widely believed that sluggers have an unfair advantage these days because of juiced base-balls, smaller ballparks, and subpar pitching.

Besides making a name for himself, Bell played a part in helping Jackie Robinson enter the major leagues. Robinson crossed major league baseball's color line in 1946. Brooklyn Dodgers' owner Branch Rickey felt that Robinson would be able to tolerate the racism and pressure he would be subjected to in the major leagues. Robinson was subjected to threats and ridicule throughout his career. In his first season, the pressure forced him into a slump, but he did recover and ended up having an impressive career that earned him a spot in the Major League Baseball Hall of Fame in Cooperstown, New York.

When Robinson finally did make it to the Brooklyn Dodgers on opening day in 1947, he became the first African American to do so in over fifty years. It was not only a monumental day for Robinson, it was a monumental day for Bell, too. African Americans had finally been given a chance to prove that they could hit, catch, and run with anyone in the major leagues.

Bell took time to do whatever he could to help Robinson and other African American players make it into the major leagues. Robinson and Bell played together for a short period on the Kansas City Monarchs. When Robinson finally got the opportunity to start that fateful spring day in 1947, Bell said it was the greatest day of his life.

While scouts were eyeing Robinson and considering him for the major leagues in 1946, Bell was competing with Monte Irvin for the

Negro National League batting title. Bell felt that he was too old to make the transition at that time. Major league club owners still wanted Negro league players to go through the minor leagues, and Bell felt that he just didn't have enough time to go through that. So in 1946, he threw the batting title so Irvin could take it. Scouts noticed how Irvin won the batting title that year, and it helped him to be picked to play for the New York Giants.

While it is widely believed that Robinson was the first black man to play in the major leagues, this is not true. Moses Fleetwood Walker was the first Negro major leaguer. Walker began playing professional ball in 1883 for Toledo, Ohio. When Toledo left the Northwestern League to enter the American Association the following year, Walker went with the team and at that point became the first African American to play in the major leagues.

Fans' reactions to Walker were mixed. He was well received in the North, where sportswriters saluted him for making valuable

Chicago American Giant Cool Papa Bell *(left)* **watches the action on the field with manager Candy Jim Taylor during a Negro National League game against the New York Black Yankees on July 26, 1942.**

contributions to the Toledo team. But in the South, things were different. In September of 1884, shortly before Toledo headed to Richmond, Virginia, for a three-game series, Toledo manager Charlie Morton received a letter from Richmond:

> We the undersigned do hereby warn you not to put up Walker, the Negro catcher, the evenings that you play in Richmond, as we could mention the names of 75 determined men who have sworn to mob Walker if he comes on the ground in a suit. We hope you will listen to our words of warning, so that there will be no trouble; but if you do not there certainly will be. We only write this to prevent much bloodshed, as you alone can prevent.

Bell and his teammates were often subjected to racist remarks. There were many hotels that they could not stay in and restaurants they could not eat in because of the color of their skin. Road life was tough, on the field and off.

Entire teams would sometimes travel 100 miles or more in one car to get to a game, and then 100 miles back—all in the same day. In some towns, especially in the South, they would be denied food and drink in restaurants once they got to the town they were scheduled to play in.

When Bell played for the Pittsburgh Crawfords, he and the team would often travel all night in their bus to make it to the next game. The summer heat and long hours were tough on the team, but they still managed to win most of their games. Bell said that they had to learn how to sleep "lying down, sitting, or standing up."

When they were able to stop for rest, they often encountered discrimination. Once, the Crawfords were barred from using the showers in the clubhouse of a stadium they played at in Ohio. Rumor has it that they convinced a woman who owned a rooming house to fill a bathtub with water so they could clean up. Nine players cleaned themselves in the same tub. Getting food was a struggle as well. There was one night when Crawfords players could not find a single restaurant between Akron and Youngstown, Ohio, that would cook for them. Even when they had money, it was hard to find service.

The players would have to pack food along with their gloves, uniforms, bats, and hats. But this didn't always solve the problem. The players who prepared food for themselves often had it stolen by the players who didn't. One pitcher for the Crawfords, Harry Kincannon, is said to have guarded his food with a pistol. "Anybody eatin' my food tonight is gonna get it with this," he warned his teammates. Once, after Kincannon fell asleep, one of the Crawfords picked up the pistol and removed the bullets. The Crawfords then ransacked Kincannon's bag and passed his food around. After they were done, they draped the leftovers all over him. Kincannon was obviously angry, but he laughed about it with the team when he woke up.

As a result of discriminatory practices, many African American players preferred to play

President Rafael L. Trujillo of the Dominican Republic lured a number of Negro league players, including Cool Papa Bell, to play for his team in 1937.

winter ball in Latin America during the off-season. They were treated better, earned more money, and were shown respect there.

In 1937, while at spring training for the Pittsburgh Crawfords in New Orleans, Bell's teammate Satchel Paige went to play for President Rafael L. Trujillo's baseball team in the Dominican Republic. Trujillo was preparing for an upcoming election. His opponent had imported a ball club that was beating up on almost every club in the Dominican Republic. The nation was in a baseball craze, and at that time a politician's popularity—and chance for reelection—depended heavily on what kind of baseball team he could put in the field. In his bid for reelection, Trujillo sought to build a top-notch team. He wanted Paige and Bell to play for him. This is what Bell said about Satchel's inability to avoid the money offered to him by Trujillo:

> They liked baseball down there. They had a championship series set down there, and they said if Trujillo would win they

would put him back in office: He was
pretty near out of office then. So they got
guys from Cuba, Panama, and guys out of
the Negro leagues—they had a lot of boys
from the States. And they wanted Satchel.
He was down in New Orleans training
with the Crawfords, and he didn't want to
go. So they trailed Satchel to a hotel in
New Orleans. Someone told them Satchel
was in there. So two of them went in to
look for him, and Satchel slipped out the
side door and jumped in his car and tried
to get away from them, but they blocked
the street and stopped him.

These were men from Santo Domingo
who were looking for ballplayers to take
down there. Now Satchel was the type of
guy that if you showed him money—or a
car—you could lead him anywhere. He
was that type of fella. He did a lot of wrong
things in baseball, but he was easily led.
So they said they wanted him to go down
there, and he said, "I don't wanna go."

He had been out in North Dakota already and run off from our team. And we bought a boy from St. Louis named Vincent, and we swapped Vincent out in North Dakota to bring Paige back to the league. So when Vincent went out there and Paige came back to the league, he didn't want to jump again. That's why he was ducking those people. But when they offered him a big salary, then he jumped again and went down there.

In all, nine men from the Pittsburgh Crawfords, including Bell, headed down to the Dominican Republic that year. The best thing about playing *beisbol* in Cuba, Mexico, Puerto Rico, Venezuela, and other Latin American countries was the absence of discrimination and the color line. Whites played with blacks and Hispanics. It also showed how silly the color line was. In Latin American countries, it was obvious that the color of a man's skin had no effect on his ability to play baseball.

Willie Wells of the Newark Eagles had fond memories of playing ball in Mexico. He began spending his summers there, too. "Not only do I get more money playing here, but I live like a king. I've found freedom and democracy here, something I never found in the United States. I was branded a Negro in the States and had to act accordingly. Everything I did, including playing ball, was regulated by my color. Well, here in Mexico, I am a man. I can go as far in baseball as I am capable of going."

But *beisbol* did have its share of hardships. In Santo Domingo, Josh Gibson, Bell, and other Crawfords joined Paige. Trujillo's team had some of the most talented players in baseball's history. But no matter how good they were, they must have feared for their lives. Trujillo told the team that they had to win, or else they would be put to death by a firing squad.

To make sure that the Crawfords knew it was no joke, the players were kept in their hotel and guarded by Trujillo's men when they were not playing. As they played, Trujillo's soldiers were in the stands, carrying rifles with bayonets. The Crawfords played well and won the championship. After winning the championship, they found out that if they had lost, Trujillo's army might have been overthrown, and they might not have ever escaped the country.

Hall of Famer Cool Papa Bell presents Lou Brock of the St. Louis Cardinals with a base after Brock broke the single season stolen-base record with his 105th steal during a game between the Cardinals and the Philadelphia Phillies on September 10, 1994.

5 After Baseball

At the age of forty-five, after spending twenty-four years in the professional Negro leagues, Bell retired from pro ball and began playing for the Detroit Senators, an all-black semipro independent team. It was the last team he played for.

Before retiring from baseball, Bell endured the death of his friend and Crawfords teammate Josh Gibson. Gibson died in 1947. He was only thirty-six years old. Cool Papa had fond memories of Gibson's exploits. "One year Gibson hit 72 home runs that I counted," Bell said. "He would hit more if all the parks had been fenced in like in the majors. Sometimes the outfielders got back 500 feet and Gibson would still hit the ball over their heads. Have you ever heard of a 500-foot out? But we'd play two, sometimes three games a day and he would be tired and just couldn't run out those long hits."

During an exhibition game in Yankee Stadium, it is said that Gibson hit a ball out of the stadium. Not just over the fence, but all the way over the back wall that separates the park from the rest of the Bronx. Bell and others said that they heard about the mammoth shot, but none of them actually saw it. Gibson himself never made the claim, but the story still remains a legend in baseball lore. The story was important to African American ballplayers because it meant that Gibson was able to hit the ball farther than Babe Ruth. Gibson was compared to Ruth throughout his career, and the idea that Gibson was getting credit for something Ruth never accomplished helped many African American ballplayers feel that Gibson was finally getting the credit he deserved.

"He was a good catcher, too. Smart," Bell said of Gibson. "He threw a light ball to second. You could catch it bare-handed. Some catchers throw a brick down to second."

Satchel Paige and Josh Gibson played on the same teams for much of their careers, but they did oppose each other while barnstorming. Paige said that Gibson was the best hitter he ever faced, even better than Bell. "You look for his weakness and while you lookin' for it he liable to hit forty-five home runs," Paige said.

The biggest difference between Bell, Paige, and Gibson was that the years of struggling to survive in the Negro leagues burned Gibson out. By 1941, when he was only thirty, Gibson started getting dizzy while chasing after pop-ups. Gibson was a catcher, and it began taking its toll on his knees. He lost a lot of his speed and stopped stealing bases.

By 1942, Gibson was still swatting balls over fences with ease, but it seemed like he was beginning to tire. He complained of painful headaches and turned to alcohol to ease the pain. Gibson had come down with hypertension (high blood pressure), a very serious medical condition. His drinking only made it worse, and the condition had horrible effects on his health and playing ability.

Gibson was still one of the Negro league's premiere hitters in 1943, but in 1944 he hit just six home runs in thirty-nine games. Off the field, he was getting sicker. He went into depression, was hospitalized for uncontrollable fits of anger, and threatened to commit suicide.

Gibson appeared in his last East-West All-Star Game in 1946. He suffered a stroke in January of 1947 while at a movie theater and died the same day. His death shocked Cool Papa Bell and other African American baseball players. It made them wonder if Gibson's unstable mental condition had something to do with the discrimination he endured and the fact that he never made it into the major leagues.

Most Negro league players learned to live with the color line. But Gibson knew that he was one of the greatest sluggers to ever play baseball, and he had been told many times about how much money he could make in the major leagues. In 1942, when major league club owners spent more time scouting Negro league players, Gibson was told by Bill Benswanger, the Pittsburgh Pirates owner, that he was being considered for a major league contract. But the contract never came.

"He was a big, overgrown boy," Jimmie Crutchfield said of Gibson. "He was such a nice guy. But it bothered him that he wasn't going to make the big leagues. It really did. To me it seems that Josh died of a broken heart."

Bell had a photograph of Gibson holding a bat at Griffith Stadium in Washington, D.C. Fans had given him the bat. The words "Josh the Basher" were painted on the bat. "I don't care what league or where it was, Josh hit the long ball more often than any other player I've ever seen. Anyone!" Bell said.

In 1948, the year after Gibson died, Tom Baird and J. L. Wilkinson, who were co-owners of the Kansas City Monarchs, called on Bell and hired him to manage their minor league team. The contract was written so that Bell's team was called the Kansas City Stars or the Kansas City Travelers when they were playing near Kansas City. When they played outside the midwestern United States, the team was called the Kansas City Monarchs.

Bell managed the team until 1950. In those three seasons, Bell coached Ernie Banks and Elston Howard. Both Howard and Banks went on to become major league stars. Banks said that Bell was responsible for taking him from the Texas sandlots to Kansas City. Both Lou Brock and Maury Wills say that Bell played a part in teaching them the art of base stealing.

It is said that Bell was offered a job to play for the major league St. Louis Browns club in 1948, but he turned it down. By that time, he was already forty-five years old and way past his prime.

Baseball did not leave Bell rich. There were no pensions for Negro league ballplayers, so

The Los Angeles Dodgers' Maury Wills, shown here stealing second base, credits Cool Papa Bell for helping him develop his base-running skills.

Bell had to continue working. After he ended his playing and coaching career, he worked as a custodian for city hall in St. Louis. He was promoted to night watchman of city hall and ended up working for the city for twenty-one years. He retired in 1973.

Bell spent his remaining thirty-five years in a solid red-bick duplex at 3034 Dickson Street in St. Louis, Missouri. He and his wife, Clara, lived off of the meager income provided by Social Security checks, a pension from the city of St. Louis, and a stipend from the baseball commissioner's office. In recognition of Bell's contributions to the city of St. Louis and the game of baseball, Dickson Street was renamed James Cool Papa Bell Avenue in the 1980s.

Bell said much of his inspiration to excel in baseball came from his wife, Clara. He married Clara Belle Thompson in 1928 in East St. Louis, Missouri. They were married for sixty-two years when Clara died on January 20, 1991.

Already afflicted with glaucoma, Bell suffered a heart attack on February 27, 1991. He was hospitalized at St. Louis University Hospital and died a week later on March 7, 1991. He was eighty-eight years old.

In Satchel Paige's book *Maybe I'll Pitch Forever,* Paige summed up Bell's incredible career. "If Cool Papa had known about colleges or if colleges had known about Cool Papa, Jesse Owens would have looked like he was walking."

Bell is buried at St. Peter's Cemetery in St. Louis. He never showed any bitterness or hostility about not being able to play in the major leagues. "Funny, but I don't have any regrets about not playing in the majors. At that time the doors were not open only in baseball, but in other avenues that we couldn't enter. They say that I was born too soon. I say the doors were opened up too late."

He never showed any resentment toward the all-white major leagues. It did not appear that he held any grudges for the discrimination

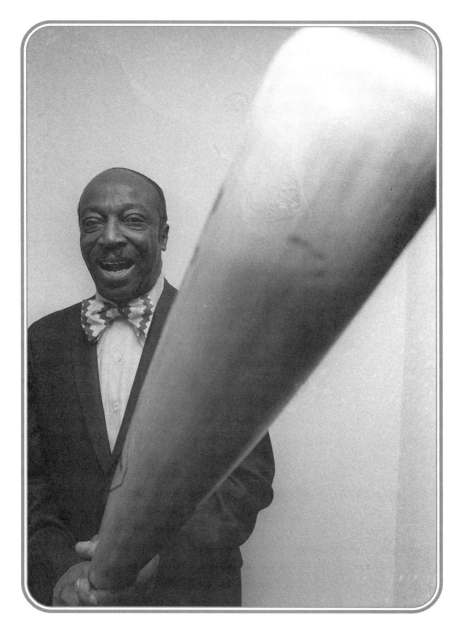

Cool Papa Bell poses with a bat after his induction into the
Baseball Hall of Fame on February 14, 1974.

he endured. In his will, he wrote that he wanted to have twelve pallbearers: six black and six white.

"Because of baseball, I smelled the rose of life," Bell said. "I wanted to meet interesting people, to travel, and to have nice clothes. Baseball allowed me to do all those things, and most important, during my time with the Crawfords, it allowed me to become a member of a brotherhood of friendship which will last forever."

Cool Papa Bell *(front left)* with Mickey Mantle *(behind Bell)*, Whitey Ford *(back right)*, and Joco Conlan *(front right)* after being inducted into the Baseball Hall of Fame on August 12, 1974.

The Hall
of Fame

Cool Papa Bell was elected to the National
Baseball Hall of Fame in Cooperstown,
New York, on August 12, 1974. He was
the fifth Negro league star to be inducted at
Cooperstown. His St. Louis Stars' uniform
and a plaque that describes his career are
showcased there today.

The other Negro league players who have
made it into the Hall of Fame are Willie
Foster, Satchel Paige, Josh Gibson, Buck
Leonard, Monte Irvin, Judy Johnson, Oscar
Charleston, Martin Dihigo, John Henry Lloyd,
Rube Foster, Ray Dandridge, and Leon Day.
The coming years will certainly bring more.

Walter F. "Buck" Leonard was born in September 1907. In his prime he was one of the Negro leagues' most feared sluggers. Between 1937 and 1946, he and home-run legend Josh Gibson were the most dangerous 3–4 combination in the Negro league. Leonard was a five-foot-eleven-inch, 185-pound lefty slugger. He had a graceful swing that brought him many long, long hits. He played first base for the Homestead Grays, one of the greatest teams in Negro league history. After leaving baseball, Buck went to work for the city of Rocky Mount, North Carolina, as an assistant probation officer. He died in 1997.

Many Negro league players felt that Willie Foster was the best left-handed pitcher they ever faced. Foster featured a blazing fastball and a sharp breaking ball. He was known as much for his finesse and intelligence on the mound as he was for his ability to overpower hitters. He would lull hitters to sleep with off-speed breaking pitches and then shock them with a speeding fastball. Between 1923 and

Josh Gibson in a catcher's uniform on the field for the
Homestead Grays

1938, he played for various semipro teams, the Memphis Red Sox, and the Chicago American Giants.

Monte Irvin, like many great African American athletes of his time, played most of his career in the Negro leagues. He did make it to the major leagues—with Bell's help—and he played an important role during his eight seasons with the New York Giants. The Giants won two pennants with Irvin. Irvin started his professional baseball career in the Negro leagues at the age of seventeen. He developed into a power-hitting, smooth-fielding, base-stealing triple threat. In 1951, Irvin stole home in the World Series. He was inducted into the Hall of Fame in 1973.

Judy Johnson was a fixture at third base for the Negro National League's Hilldale club in the 1920s and 1930s. His contemporaries felt he was one of the smartest and slickest fielders in the game. In the first Negro World Series in 1924, he led Hilldale's hitting attack with a .341 batting average. After retiring, he became a major league baseball scout.

Oscar Charleston was a mighty hitter over his forty-year career. Between 1915 and 1954, Charleston played for the Indianapolis ABCs, the Harrisburg Giants, the Homestead Grays, the Pittsburgh Crawfords, the Philadelphia Stars, and the Indianapolis Clowns. Charleston played first base and center field, and also managed teams. Oscar had running speed, power at the plate, and a powerful throwing arm. Charleston is said to have hit over .400 five times in his career. His lifetime average is .357. Jimmie Crutchfield, who played under Charleston on the Pittsburgh Crawfords, said, "If I had to pick the best player I saw in my time, it would be hard to pick between Charleston and Josh Gibson. When the chips were down and you needed somebody to bat in the clutch—even at his age Charleston was as good as anybody playing baseball."

Martin Dihigo was a stellar performer at whatever position he played—pitching, infield, or outfield. Buck Leonard called Dihigo the best ballplayer of all time. Dihigo first played

John Henry "Pop" Lloyd, considered one of baseball's greatest shortstops, had a career batting average of over .300. He was inducted into the Hall of Fame in 1977.

professional ball in America in 1923, when he was just fifteen years old. He often started games in center field and later came on to pitch in relief. In 1929, he was credited with hitting .386 in the American Negro League. Along with Cool Papa Bell, Satchel Paige, Josh Gibson, and others, he played several seasons in Latin America in the 1930s and 1940s.

John Henry "Pop" Lloyd played shortstop for at least five different professional Negro league teams: the Philadelphia Giants, the New York Lincoln Giants, the Chicago American Giants, the Brooklyn Royal Giants, and the Atlantic City Bacharach Giants. Most of his contemporaries say that he was the greatest shortstop ever. Even Honus Wagner, his white rival at shortstop, admitted this. Lloyd's career batting average is .339.

Andrew "Rube" Foster is said to have been the best pitcher of his time, black or white. Rube played twenty-four years for the Chicago American Giants between 1902 and 1926. He is credited with starting the Negro National

League, the strongest of all the Negro leagues. Foster was a huge man. He weighed about 300 pounds. He was one of the greatest managers ever. As a pitcher, Rube once went 54 and 1 in a season. As a manager, he once led his team to a 126 and 6 record. He is also credited with inventing little ball, the art that Bell perfected and that African American baseball players brought back to the major leagues when Jackie Robinson began playing for the Brooklyn Dodgers in 1947.

Ray Dandridge came very close to making the major leagues. He was a sixteen-year Negro league veteran when the Minneapolis Millers of the Triple-A American Association signed him in 1949. He was already in his forties, but he hit .362 in his first year with the Millers. He batted .311 the next year and was named the league's Most Valuable Player. Dandridge quit the Millers after the 1951 season, when he hit .324. After retiring from baseball, he began work as a talent scout for the San Francisco Giants.

Leon Day may have been the most outstanding pitcher in the Negro National League during the late 1930s and early 1940s. He was the ace of the Newark Eagles' pitching staff. Day's vicious curveball and sneaky fastball, which he delivered with a no-windup, sidearm motion, helped him earn impressive strikeout records. In 1937, Leon was 13 and 0 in league play and batted .320. He also played two winters in Cuba and one in Venezuela (going 12 and 1), and three summers in Mexico.

Between 1935 and 1946, Day appeared in a record seven East-West All-Star Games. In the 1942 game, he set a Negro league record when he struck out eighteen Baltimore batters in one game. He once was recruited by the Homestead Grays to oppose Satchel Paige in the Negro World Series and struck out twelve batters in a 4–1 victory. He played until 1955.

Timeline

1901 James Thomas Bell is born near Starkville, Mississippi.

1910 First efforts to establish a national Negro baseball league fail.

1920 The first viable Negro National League, with eight teams, is established. In the same year, Bell leaves Mississippi and settles in St. Louis, Missouri, where he signs on with the Compton Hill Cubs.

1921 Bell completes his first full season with the St. Louis Stars, batting over .400.

1933 Bell begins a four-year stint with the Pittsburgh Crawfords. Bell claims to have stolen 175 bases in 200 games during the 1933 season.

1937 Bell travels to the Dominican Republic and plays for the baseball team of dictator Rafael Trujillo.

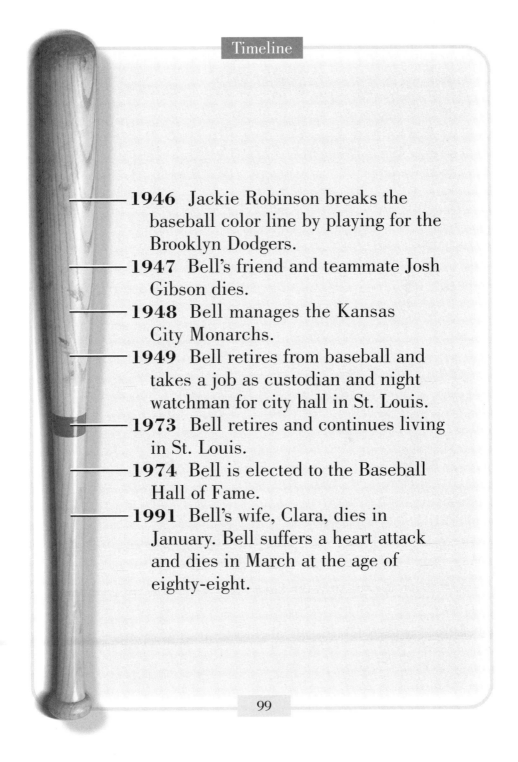

1946 Jackie Robinson breaks the baseball color line by playing for the Brooklyn Dodgers.

1947 Bell's friend and teammate Josh Gibson dies.

1948 Bell manages the Kansas City Monarchs.

1949 Bell retires from baseball and takes a job as custodian and night watchman for city hall in St. Louis.

1973 Bell retires and continues living in St. Louis.

1974 Bell is elected to the Baseball Hall of Fame.

1991 Bell's wife, Clara, dies in January. Bell suffers a heart attack and dies in March at the age of eighty-eight.

Glossary

barnstormer A player who travels from town to town to play baseball.

batting A hitter's ability to make contact with the baseball.

bunt A ball that is hit very softly. When bunting, hitters do not swing. They hold the bat parallel to the ground in an attempt to bounce the ball a few feet in front of home plate.

change-up The opposite of a fastball. It is a slow pitch thrown with the same motion as a fastball. Change-ups are used to throw off a hitter's timing.

curveball A medium-speed pitch that drops several inches just as it approaches home plate. It is thrown with a different motion than the fastball.

double   A base hit that allows the hitter to reach second base safely.

fastball   The most common pitch, normally thrown between eighty-five and ninety-five miles per hour. Fastballs are used to set up change-ups, which are thrown with the same motion as a fastball but at a much slower speed.

home run   A base hit that allows the hitter to reach home plate safely and score a run. Most home runs are hit out of the ballpark, but occasionally a hitter is able to run around the bases and slide into home plate before being tagged with the baseball.

inning   Baseball games are divided into nine innings. There are six outs in each inning: three outs for the home team and three outs for the visiting team.

juiced ball   A tightly wound baseball that travels farther and faster than a normal baseball after it is hit.

knuckleball   A pitch that is gripped with a pitcher's knuckles and thrown softly toward the plate without any rotation. Knuckleballs tend to dart up, down, left, or right as they approach the plate.

lead off   The first hitter to bat in an inning.

little ball   A baseball strategy in which walks, stolen bases, bunting, and sacrifice hits are very important.

rookie   A first-year baseball player.

sacrifice   A batter who gives up his at-bat by hitting the ball so runners can move over to second or third base. Sacrifices are used when there are less than two outs to increase a team's chances of scoring a run.

shadowball   A warm-up exercise where players pitch, hit, throw, and catch an imaginary baseball.

slugging   A hitter's strength or ability to hit the ball hard and far.

southpaw   A left-handed pitcher.

stolen base   A base that is taken by a speedy runner. A runner steals by running from one base to the next after a pitch is thrown. The runner must slide safely into the base before the catcher can throw him out in order to steal the base.

strike   A ball that is swung on and missed or thrown within the edges of home plate between the batter's knees and chest. Batters are given three strikes before they are called out.

switch hitter   A batter who bats from both the right and left sides of home plate.

triple   A base hit in which the batter reaches third base safely.

veteran   An experienced baseball player who has played for several years.

For More Information

Organizations

A. Bartlett Giamatti Research Center
National Baseball Hall of Fame Library
25 Main Street
P.O. Box 590
Cooperstown, NY 13326
(607) 547-0330
(607) 547-0335
Web site: http://baseballhalloffame.org/library/
    research.htm

**Hall of Fame Film, Video, and Recorded
    Sound Department**
National Baseball Hall of Fame Library
25 Main Street

P.O. Box 590
Cooperstown, NY 13326
(607) 547-0314
Web site: http://baseballhalloffame.org/
library/fvrs.htm

The Society for American Baseball Research (SABR)

812 Huron Road, Suite 719
Cleveland, OH 44115
(216) 575-0500
e-mail: info@sabr.org
Web site: http://www.sabr.org

Web Sites

Baseball Almanac
http://www.baseballalmanac.com/players/
p_bell0.shtml

Baseball-Reference.com
http://www.baseballreference.com/b/
bellco99.shtml

Biography of James "Cool Papa" Bell
http://www.ericenders.com/coolpapa.htm

Black Baseball's Negro Baseball Leagues
http://www.blackbaseball.com/players/
  bellpapa.htm

Cool Papa Bell—The Baseball Online Library
http://web2.sportsline.com/u/baseball/bol/
  ballplayers/B/Bell_Cool_Papa.html

National Baseball Hall of Fame and Museum
http://baseballhalloffame.org

Negro League Baseball
http://www.negroleaguebaseball.com

Shadowball . . . Recalling the Negro Leagues
http://www.negro-league.columbus.oh.us/
  players.htm

For Further Reading

Brashler, William. *The Story of Negro League Baseball.* New York: Ticknor & Fields, 1994.

Chadwick, Bruce. *When the Game Was Black and White.* New York: Abbeville Press, 1992.

Craft, David. *The Negro Leagues.* New York: Crescent Books, 1993.

Holway, John B. *Voices from the Great Black Baseball Leagues.* New York: Dodd, Mead & Company, 1975.

O'Connor, Jim. *Jackie Robinson and the Story of All-Black Baseball.* Toronto: Random House of Canada, 1989.

Peterson, Robert. *Only the Ball Was White.* Englewood Cliffs, NJ: Prentice-Hall, 1970.

Rogosin, Donn. *Invisible Men: Life in Baseball's Negro Leagues*. New York: Atheneum, 1983.

Tygiel, Jules. *Baseball's Great Experiment: Jackie Robinson and His Legacy*. New York: Oxford University Press, 1983.

Winter, Jonah. *Fair Ball!* New York: Scholastic Press, 1999.

Index

C

Charleston, Oscar, 25–26, 62, 89, 93

Chicago American Giants, 15, 21, 22, 61, 95

Civil War, 9, 10, 11,

Cleveland Indians, 31, 51, 55

Cobb, Ty, 17, 25, 51

color line in baseball, 6, 63

Crutchfield, Jimmie, 48, 81, 93

Cuban Giants, 13

D

Dandridge, Ray, 89, 96

Day, Leon, 89, 97

Detroit Senators, 61

Detroit Wolves, 61

Dihigo, Martin, 89, 93, 95

DiMaggio, Joe, 51

Dominican Republic, 56, 71–75

E

East-West All-Star Game, 61, 80, 97

F

Foster, Andrew "Rube," 15–18, 89, 95–96

Foster, Willie, 90, 92

G

Gatewood, Bill, 26

"Giants" as a baseball team name, 15

Gibson, Josh, 7, 32, 35, 51, 57, 59, 62, 74, 77–81, 89, 93, 95

H

Henderson, Ricky, 44

Homestead Grays, 7, 35, 61, 93, 97

I

Indianapolis Clowns, 5, 93

integration of baseball, 48, 55, 63–65

Irvin, Monte, 64–65, 89, 92

J

Jim Crow laws, 10–11

Johnson, Judy, 36, 89, 92

K

Kansas City Monarchs, 15, 22–23, 32, 56, 57, 61, 64, 82

Keeler, Willie, 51

Kincannon, Harry, 69

Ku Klux Klan, 39

L

Latin America, 56, 71–75, 95

Leonard, Buck, 35, 89, 90, 93

About the Author

Shaun McCormack is a twenty-five-year-old writer living in Brooklyn, New York. He has been a baseball fanatic since his grandfather took him to Yankee Stadium for the first time in 1980, when he was five years old.

Photo Credits

Cover, pp. 4, 16, 27, 45, 58, 66, 70, 76, 83, 91 © Corbis; pp. 8, 12, 19, 39 © Hulton Archive; pp. 24, 33, 49, 50, 53, 86, 88, 94 © AP/Wide World Photos; pp. 34, 37, 42–43, 60 © New York Public Library.

Series Design

Claudia Carlson

Layout

Nelson Sá